CROSSING OVER

MARY BURRITT CHRISTIANSEN POETRY SERIES
Hilda Raz, *Series Editor*

The Mary Burritt Christiansen Poetry Series publishes
two to four books a year that engage and give voice to the
realities of living, working, and experiencing the West and
the Border as places and as metaphors. The purpose of the
series is to expand access to, and the audience for, quality
poetry, both single volumes and anthologies, that can be
used for general reading as well as in classrooms.

Mary Burritt
Christiansen
Poetry Series

Also available in the Mary Burritt Christiansen Poetry Series:

Heresies: Poems by Orlando Menes
Self-Portrait with Spurs and Sulfur: Poems by Casey Thayer
Report to the Department of the Interior: Poems by Diane Glancy
The Arranged Marriage: Poems by Jehanne Dubrow
The Sky Is Shooting Blue Arrows: Poems by Glenna Luschei
A Selected History of Her Heart: Poems by Carole Simmons Oles
The Goldilocks Zone by Kate Gale
Flirt by Noah Blaustein
Progress on the Subject of Immensity by Leslie Ullman
Losing the Ring in the River by Marge Saiser

For additional titles in the Mary Burritt Christiansen Poetry Series,
please visit unmpress.com.

CROSSING OVER

poems

Priscilla Long

UNIVERSITY OF NEW MEXICO PRESS | ALBUQUERQUE

© 2015 by Priscilla Long
All rights reserved. Published 2015
Printed in the United States of America
20 19 18 17 16 15   1 2 3 4 5 6

Library of Congress Cataloging-in-Publication Data
Long, Priscilla.
  [Poems. Selections]
  Crossing over : poems / Priscilla Long.
       pages cm. — (Mary Burritt Christiansen Poetry Series)
  Includes bibliographical references.
  ISBN 978-0-8263-2396-5 (pbk. : alk. paper) — ISBN 978-0-8263-3706-1 (electronic)
  I. Title.
  PS3612.O5243A6 2015
  811'.6—dc23
                          2014036088

Cover illustration: "Murray Morgan and Downtown,"
photograph courtesy of Scott Hingst
Author photograph courtesy of Tony Ober
Cover designed by Felicia Cedillos
Composed in Dante MT 11.5/13.5
Display fonts are Serlio LT and Apollo MT

The self must be a bridge, not a pit.

—THEODORE ROETHKE

Contents

3. Susanne's Teapot

4. The Gong Strikes Its Own Hour

I
Memory's Load

Sister Ghost

Your beauty stuns, but
it's static, photographic.
Your stories stir the dust,
stick to the broom.
Your drawings dream
your fine-stitched quilt.
Your death—your gift
of stones to us. No blame.
Suicides are deranged
with despair. Oh Susanne.
Were there a bridge back to you,
I would take it anywhere.

Queen of the Cut

Cable-stayed bridge, Tacoma, Washington

Night-gem, sun-brooch, sky-jewel.
A phantom ship—tall-masted, cable-rigged.
Kandinsky bird in blue air.
Spare. Neat as a girl-queen
above the cut. Tacoma's quarrel
with rust and rotten brick.
She reigns, angles of gleams,
smoke-daughter, penumbra
of Mount Tacoma. Snow-peaks
dream her tides, her white piers.
She wends her wheel-trail
through ribbons of light and steel.

NOTE: In Pacific Northwest nomenclature a "cut" is a canal.

Psalm to Stones

You set me down
in a desert of stones,
you crowned me
Queen of Stones,
and so I praise
cold stones, broken
off the mother-rock,
windswept to orphan shores.
I praise stone caverns,
bat-ridden and dark,
black basalt
worn smooth as skin.
I praise the bellystone
of Buddha, the burn
of Buddha's breath.
I praise your smoke-blue eyes.
I praise the dropstone
that rides the glacier down,
the tombstone's hoard.
I do not neglect
the smaller stones:
bloodstone, lodestone,
lapis-lazuli dagger gem.
And I do not neglect my heart,
ice-glittered, jagged sharp.

Elegy for Susanne

> And I am here to burn for you like a black candle.
> —Osip Mandelstam

In a black-and-white photograph
you sit in nutmeg sun.
An odor of allspice
anoints the autumn air . . .
your husband's voice, alto
notes and flutes

before the insect schizophrenia
gnaws the pulse from thought
to dream. Fear breaks
loose, tangles with voice.
You go mute,
drug-thick, alone.

One day, you are lost.
We search the cities and towns,
the dark wood,
till hunters mistake your bones
for the white belly of a deer.

Your hair was dun, sunlight
slant on old barn planks.
Your eyes—sky and malachite.

In colors of ash and bone
your serene beauty is enough
to make a stranger stare.
You sit in nutmeg sun.
The heart-shaped leaves are falling.

Memory's Load

Eleventh Street Bridge, Tacoma, opened February 15, 1913
Renamed Murray Morgan Bridge, May 21, 1997

No miracle, this vertical-lift
steel-truss bridge, its birds,
its timbered deck built to bear
a load of workers walking
to tideflats—horses, carts, old Tacoma
streetcars. Two towers on piers
on piles pipe water over the lift-span
lifting to let pass tugboat, steamship,
barge, or bark. And years pass.
The truss turns to rust. Struts
like old bones carry memory's load:
Murray Morgan tending the lift-
motor in the lift-house bolted
to the lift-span, raising and lowering
himself, writing *Skid Road*
through ups and downs.
Now falcons roost in the old towers.
They swoop and dive, defy
geometries of rivet and steel.

History

While I with my fingertips
map the country
of your bony limbs,
tell me the history
of your desires,
wind me along
your childhood roads,
sing a scrap of lullaby.
While I curl in your body's cave,
tell me an old tale, the night
you slept hammock-high
in the redwoods
like a wild nesting bird.
While I walk in the valley
of petroglyph and shadow,
turn me in the grotto
of your sleep, where history
is not. Could never be.

Thief of Fire

In your darkest hour
I am the language you learn.
My keys fit your lock.
My fingers slit purse-silk
to pinch a nest of coins
thick with your scent.
I mount your dreaming,
kindle your sleep.
In this mirrored moonlight
you are young.
I have no scars.

My Old Flame

We lay on a yellow rug,
elbows on pillows.
I'd been touching you
all summer. At the carnival
I brushed your muscled arm.
On the Ferris wheel my fingertip
tapped your collarbone.
In a tavern I kept smoothing
your smooth cotton shirt.
Your woodworker's hands—
long-fingered, skilled . . .

In the paper lantern's glow
talk drifted between us, easy
and slow. It grew late.
Time stopped. You stood up.
I grabbed your leg. "Don't go!"
"I'm going," you said sweetly,
"to the bathroom."

You returned to our cave of light
and we talked and talked
before we began kissing,
our hearts racing,
your taut body, its muscled rises,
soft hollows, tender swells
dissolving into my own.

Winter turned the coin.
In my cold flat the roof
leaked into pans.
I trudged to a gray job,
shivered home past your street,
counted pennies, drank.

It was all so long ago.
But tonight, reading Cavafy's
Alexandrian poems, *his* old flames,
it's the gardenias I remember
tending those summer nights—
their intoxicating perfume.

After Meditation

Memory's crook lets slip
love's sack of bile—books
half-read, a stale kiss,
passion's rust, its ash.
Outside the ashram, night
winks Seattle. I walk
where cougars once roamed
full of animal grace.
I remember your wet eyes.
I remember your fire.

Body Poem

After death the writer's body
inhabits the body of work.
The eye remains,
the hand everywhere in notebooks,
the heart in beat and rasp of poem.

Voice, breast, breath,
the intricate vulva devolving
into throb, blood hot,
or not. The naked foot
dancing, leaping,
all in the body of work.

What Remains

One year, Susanne,
by chance or circumstance
I move to the green wet
of your Northwest.
These chill days of rain
I wear your purple coat
snapped shut. I splash
your streets and breathe
your spruce and pine.
I read your books—Tolstoy
and Nin. Your mountain
rises still in cedar-mist. I hear
the flap and caw of crows,
the cry of gulls. Puget Sound
is mine now. I have your voice
on tape, your photo on my wall,
its ice blue eyes. I have it all.

2

Why the Fremont Bridge and the Aurora Bridge Don't Speak

Seasonal Affective Disorder

Dark early and dark late,
Seattle squats metallic, ice-
cold rain. I'm on the bus.
Below the bascule bridge
a log-barge blocks the cut.
Too near, two women wizened
to chalk, small-talk the traffic-stuck
route to town. Downtown
I go to the museum to muse
in Morris Louis light.

Flame flares in blue air.
Mint rises to violet, to rose
gauze or smoke. I am
log, earth, mud.
This is no painting, but fire
opal, opalescent desire.
I paddle the slow green river of childhood.
Color is reason to live.

High Road Home

Aurora Bridge, Seattle, dedicated February 22, 1932

Do bridges dream their suicides?
Bodies like birds, brief,
a bright flash, then gone.
The bridge trembles
over still waters that split
spirit from falling flesh.

Blue clay holds the footing,
holds the logs that hold the piers.
The high road shadows
houseboat and backyard.

Do bridges dream their piers?
Do they span their own years?
The day in '32 they towed
the tall-masted ship
through the gap
in the half-built truss,
the schooner derelict
and doomed, taken out
to sea and torched.
And then the center span
drops to anchor arms,
shuts Lake Union to sail,
paddlewheel, and steam.
And America hits the road.

Traffic

Beside the blue lake, wires
crisscross the sunburst sky
and traffic stirs the wind.
The petal-mottled sidewalk
winks jewels of bright foil,
gumwrap, cigarette pack.
Beside the blue lake,
cherry trees gather butts,
parking lots, and Pepsi cups.
Blackberries tangle with tires.
And chickweed, shepherd's purse,
purslane, plantain grow
green in used car-grease.
Cottonwoods drop condoms
beside the blue lake.
Bindweed lets down its vine hair
into broken brown glass, and, yes,
bitter dock cracks the asphalt.

We Hold These Truths

The vise grip—unusually cold—
stirs the town to house tending,
to stuffing socks into sills

and jambs. We stove
our rooms, wrap pipes, stop
gapes and leaks,

nurse the old housebones.
The sudden freeze provokes
cheerful nesting noises,

house to clapboard house.
Done with pipes, we snug
with book, quilt, and cat. Downtown,

ice cracks brick and stone.
Three forms sleep in bags. They stick
straight out, like three good

children all tucked in,
highrise for headboard.
Above, their flag is flying.

The cold stars shine
on three old men. Over two
breath whitens the cruel air.

Why the Fremont Bridge and the Aurora Bridge Don't Speak

They've stood side by side
for so long. The Fremont Bridge, bascule
built 1917, is older, lower, smaller.
It's had its ups and downs.
The Aurora Bridge is superior.
When it opened—1932—thousands came
to cheer. They ignored, even stood upon
the older, lower bridge. The Fremont
Bridge moans its horn day and night,
its paint fading, its mesh deck
decrepit, dotted with pigeon poop.
But the old bridge has a tender.
And now, an artist in residence
to climb its little tower.
The Aurora Bridge is the jumper's
bridge. Beauty debated and hated.
The Fremont Bridge, cracked,
grumpy, groaning, is loved.
That's why they don't speak.

Pantoum for a Pontoon Bridge

Hood Canal Floating Bridge, built 1961
Western half sank during a severe storm, February 13, 1979

Hood's fjord—no calm lake.
The moon hauls the dead load
to high hell. Steel cables break.
The sea's wrath takes the road.

The tide mauls the dead load.
Works of engineers collapse.
The sea's wrath takes the road,
deranges maps.

Works of engineers collapse.
The storm takes pontoons and piers,
deranges maps
and works of engineers.

The storm takes pontoons and piers
to high hell. Steel cables break
the works of engineers.
Hood's fjord is no calm lake.

Nile Valley Landslide

Yakima County, Washington, October 11, 2009

They wake to cracks, rocks
dropped, rains of gravel, the fall
of mountain sand, seabottom, dirt
of the ages. Then a basalt
boulder rolls into the river,
roaring like an animal.

The mountain moves; animals
wake and run. Immense rocks
creep down to the Naches River.
People, stunned, watch the sky fall.
A heavy rain of basalt
stops the blue river with dirt.

The Naches River, dirt-
choked, runs like a spooked animal,
flows around basalt.
Trout gasp on high rock.
The mountain rides its slow fall
into the ancient river.

So the earth moves. So the river
trespasses into pasture to get past dirt.
The mountain dances its fall
down to farms, porches, farm animals,
nature's bulldozer pushing rock
into roads turned to talus, to basalt.

Talus is broken rock, broken basalt.
Basalt once flowed, a hot river
cooling to igneous rock
lying over loose sand, the dirt
slippery. So the landslide, animal-
like, wakes and waits to fall.

Now comes October, the fall
of the great fall of basalt.
We *Homo sapiens*, brainless animal,
quarried the old rock of the river-
bank, sold the landslide toe, dirt
once pillar to mountain rock.

And so the great rocks fall
and dirt marries basalt, and the river
rages like a wounded animal.

To My Country in Time of War

Gulf War, February 1991

Rain grays Green Lake.
Wigeons paddle among rushes.
Wood ducks dabble, coots bob.
I walk around the lake telling
toad rush from bulrush from spike rush.
I nod to the weeping birch,
salute the naked larch. Raindrops
rinse my face, but my mind
keeps jangling TV jingo,
cheerful talk of smart bombs,
canned sadness for collateral damage,
brisk reports—among Advil ads—
of 200,000 dead. I'm an American,
through and through. But today
I pledge allegiance to coots.
I pledge allegiance to cudweed
and cat's-ear. I pledge allegiance
to hawkweed and horseweed and chickweed.
I pledge allegiance to ducks.

The Red Queen

Queen of war.
Queen of crack and firestorm.
She whirls in liquid flame, dances
drunken nights to doom.
She crashes cars, laughs
the lemmings down to sea.
Scorpion queen.
Queen of death by dynamite.
She spins her cobra eyes,
her beautiful cobra eyes.

PTSD Poem

1. Post-traumatic
Memory eschews chronology,
replays cartoon stars falling
from the brain's repertoire
before footfalls in the hallway,
before doorknocks
drifting through sleep
like bombs.

2. Stress
April is the cruellest month.
April's dogwood bud,
its sparrow song and weeping
birch, replay weak cries . . .
cries from nowhere . . .
thinner than air . . .

3. Disorder
Call her Medusa.
She was once a girl,
sweet as any girl,
who, raped,
turns to stone
all she looks upon.

Cliffs of Fall

Yale Bridge, Clark and Cowlitz Counties, Washington

Lewis River roils through Doug-fir
down to the Columbia.
A county road rides
the North Fork's north ledge—
cliffs of fall. O the mind,
mind has mountains . . . The road
veers to bridge earth's gash,
to leap the sheer, to run
Yale to Yacolt. Steel rope
suspends the span, spurns
the mind's abyss. Trestle
and truss recant an older bridge.
Backstays anchor to basalt.
The live load is log truck,
RV, black bear, mule deer.
The dead load—a timber deck.
Hawks nest high in steel-
tower trees. The bridge
defies earth, defines sky,
rock, river bluff, black waters
whispering to infinity.

Green River Blues

What the river says, that's what I say.
—WILLIAM STAFFORD

The Green River winds
down its gorge, whispers
chinook, coho, chum,
speaks black bear and elk,
bald eagle and blue heron.
The river slides under bridges
and past towns, past logging roads.
It slips past Black Diamond, Green
Valley Road, Green River Road,
Riverbend Road. It wends down
around Meander Park, Fort Dent,
Russell Road. The Green River
sleeps down past the Kent coalfields
through mist and dark trees
into the Duwamish. And the river
murmurs its murdered girls:
Wendy, Debbie, Mary,
Marcia, Maureen, Marie, Mary,
Constance, Carol, Kimberly,
Kimi-Kai, Carrie, Terry, Tracey,
Shawnda, Alma, Linda,
Patricia, Pammy, Patricia,
Martina, Tina, Yvonne,
Debra, Denise, Debra,
Cheryl, Shirley, Cindy, Lisa,
April, Colleen, Kelly, Delise,
Delores, Marta, Mary, Opal,
Gisele, Gail, Sandra, Cynthia,
Roberta, Andrea, Jane Doe,
Jane Doe, Jane Doe, Jane Doe.

3
Susanne's Teapot

Hot Words

Irene Drennan (d. August 23, 2008)

The dead return. Let crones
exalt their cheating ways.
Let August burn fireweed,
milkweed, bull thistle. I dream
down Latona Street past Irene's
old haunt. Old Beat poet, cursing,
laughing, composing to the grave—
I am resident lunatic here—
her Cherokee-thick, raven-black
hair turned white. *Death licks
the walls with burning.* Today
is her yahrzeit. One year dead.
Words sweep down like carrion bats.
Poet beyond wine and smoky rooms,
beyond hot blues and the phoenix
bursting into fire, do you know
how your death trails your life,
your neon Jesus, your jazz nights,
your *piss-damp alleys* and hot words?

Another Poem for Irene

Like certain old women,
autumn dances drunk.
Oxblood oaks sway and shake
naked their dark arms. Dogwood
burns to cinnabar. Sumac fire
licks the bronze evening light.

Wind ruffles the great maple
just to fiddle her crows. Birch
leaves tumble with hawthorn haws,
chestnuts with acorns.

Nothing remembers its place.

Send Word to Lorca

Send word to the jasmine
to bring its tiny whiteness.
Send word to the honeybee
to bring its busy dance.
Send word to the war
that we are tired,
that we are done with war.
Send word to the president
that we *refuse to see the blood.*
Send word to the rose
that we desire its red,
adore its thorn.
Send word to the salmon
to bring its smoked fish.
Send word to Lorca,
shot dead in Spain: his song's
still *full of sunlight and flint.*

Reading the Book of the Dead

The Field Museum of Natural History, Chicago

In these Egyptian tombs
we read the Book of the Dead.
Vanity gilds mirrors, urns,
a lapis-lazuli throne.
Beetles teem with afterlife.
A blind harper strums.

Under glass, a half-grown boy
lies embalmed to coffee black.
It is not known when he came unwrapped.
His boy's face serene, his sinews,
small hands—true to life.

We imbibe strange peace
from death come so far,
the small, light boat
to the other side,
still there, still waiting . . .

Susanne's Teapot

Ceramic blue.
Tea for us two.

Cheerful pot.
Little spout.

Blue of eyes
before demise.

Would sisters stay,
we'd gab all day.

I've something blue:
What's left of you.

Visitations

There is a land of the living and a land of the dead,
and the bridge is love . . .
—THORNTON WILDER

The dead have nothing new to say.

Susanne drops in for a glass
of Beaujolais. We drag
sister cigarettes, plot
our distant dotage: silk slippers,
sips and naps and whiskey nips.
Her death at forty
is thirty years old.
Still, she loves my poems.
Still, she'll walk the China Wall.

The dead have nothing new to say.

And Grandma Henry,
wheelchair-bent, willing
cheer. She grieves Susanne.
She re-appears to re-declaim
who begat whom
back to the twelfth century.

The dead have nothing new to say.

And Gay: girlhood
friend. I'm sixty. She's still
sixteen. Slim, she wades on river stones.
We splash and toss our seaweed hair.
We walk the dusty road.

The dead have nothing new to say.

They do not age,
but their deaths are aging.
We seldom cry for them now.
Still, on odd, solitary evenings
they come to call.
They visit, but they have lost
the art of conversation.
They repeat themselves.
They have nothing new to say.

Shadows and Dust

Derelict brick, dust-curtained
windowpanes, shadows
of branches swaying
like an old song. Nostalgia's
not history. Still, old friend,
I remember your face.
Years and wars have passed.
Mortar crumbles, shed roofs
cave. Tonight I'm reading
Akhmatova, her 800 poems
composed during Stalin's night
of terror. Back in *our* old days
we had it easy. Though not
without deaths to bear, dark
memories of kisses, lost years.

Mount Tahoma

Seattle mutters rain.
A rat corpse clots the curb.
Skyscraper glass lusters black
hawthorn drizzle, common juniper
gloom. I stump to library-days,
trip on pavement juts.
Umbrellas splay in gutters
like broken birds.
Under my burden of books,
I curse the rain
or curse the lack of rain,
whichever this is.

Then the mountain
comes out. It towers
over city towers,
immense, airy—
glacier-gauged crags.
Majesty. I see eternity.
My own dear life.

Aubade

The work of hoarding quiet
in dark mornings of rain.
Letting the mind rain.

Or reading an old book,
yellow page dreaming
blue silk, a stone Buddha.

The work of scrubbing
pots and pans, washing
the body's abode. October

rain turns asphalt to river
bottom, whispers praise
to dead orange leaves.

Kaddish for Susanne

In solitary rooms I see the dead
dance to klezmer violin.
A minor key swells
but I have spent my tears,
I have sighed
her lost loves,
I have danced her doom.
Now let gut and bent wood
keen her dark memory.

Let candleflame flicker
for the dead. Let mandolins
pluck the heartstring.

All praise to all that is.

4

The Gong Strikes Its Own Hour

Rhapsody

I walk under hot yellow skies.
The hot yellow fingers of the sun
stroke light my neck, my arms,
my salt-sweat face, stun the crows
silk-black and still. The wires sing,
the cars shining hot sing, the sand-hot
pavement sizzles and I sing the asphalt,
the steel-hot bridge, the blue lake,
white sails dazzling the dark
below the bridge. The sun hot
all in my hair tickles my arms,
tickles my back, tickles and strokes
my salt-lick face. I sing the road,
the ducks, the creosote poles.
I sing the barberries,
the burgundy-dark trees. I walk
under hot yellow skies, the sun hot,
its fingers all yellow in my hair.

Love Poem

> We ought to dream more.
> —GASTON BACHELARD

Down in the blue depths
words dream among themselves,
begin to love. Reveries
murmur in vagabond tongues,
swell the poppies to fire.

What jubilant, gentle work . . .
What bliss for the summer night!

Bluebells ding the diphthongs,
delight the red depths.
Diphthongs tongue their tender bells.
Words rub each other,
boogie-woogie and bebop, bump
and hump in blue drunkenness.

To Compose a Poem

Follow with your fingers
the hollows and hills of letters,
follow their curves
to their peaks and gurgling
wells. Keep your fingers feeling
the dips and downs,
the hills and dales of letters themselves.
Follow the fat,
loop the skin of the letters themselves.
Feel how words bump,
ding, dip, and bop
across the slippery silk.
Feel how they rush into whiteness.
Dip your fingers into their furls,
into their indigo blood.
Feel how they want
to whisper the page.
Feel them curl
to the kiss of the page.

Poet's Palette

Blue stone. Bird
in flight. Sticks and bones.

Diphthong drunk
on violet eyes.

Iron gate. Black snake.
The Dresden firestorm.

Red coal. Cedar smoke.
The golden waterfall.

Plumb bob.
Burnt orange dream.

River light. Turtle dung.
The Broken Tower.

A wild horse. A pot
of bloodshot moon.

The Poet Cleans Out Her Desk Drawer

Old poems dead
in their cases,
notebooked
like teenagers grounded.
Poems yellow about the edges,
attic lace worked long ago
by some unknown girl's fingers.
Poems forgotten even by the poet,
who may also be dead
for all these poems know,
or out dancing with some loser,
some beer-drinking fan,
some big guy who couldn't tell
a poem from pigweed or pokeweed
or any kind of weed.

Writer's Prophecy

After my death, my books
will set about reading one another,
poems puzzling over prose,

paragraphs tripping on verses.
And my characters, all rather shy,
will stumble out of their stories,

profusely excusing themselves. Rosalie
will talk too much. Simon won't answer.
Max will steal Simon's coat.

My dreams, after my death,
will coalesce into paintings
that think they are dreaming.

My bank, regretting flagrant usury,
will send each of my fortunate heirs
a gracious note of apology.

Calder

Tin and bone tickle the moon.
Bud and tendril tender
their mantra to motion,
their canticle to cosmic
convolution, cantilevered
to the curve of space-time.
Bugs and cows, cows and bugs.
A beast bolted to floorboards
curls its red tail. Dots spin like stars.
Stars quiver and dance, dither and delay.
The snake grins, the pig grunts,
the gong strikes its own hour.

NOTE: American sculptor Alexander Calder (1898–1976) invented the mobile and
made motion an integral part of his works. Calder was trained as a mechanical
engineer.

Schuyler

August. Seattle's dry but
feels like rain. The trees are dying.
I'm on the 26 going downtown
to yoga. It's 6 a.m. I ignore
brown yards and weeds. We cross
the Fremont Bridge, turn down Dexter.
I daydream Washington State,
its rivers and corners, Pacific County
bordering the Pacific Ocean. New Yorkers,
note: Seattle's not a seaside city.
Look at your map. And rain.
Manhattan rains more.
So now you know.

The bus is silent. Reading
going on. I read your poet,
that shy shill, that endearing
mess going from dapper butts
to bully barrooms, typing
in his undershorts, a little high,
a little drunk. James Schuyler—
to him I dedicate my deep bow.

Light at Arles

A sun-drenched afternoon
painted in a peacock century.
The bare room: bed, basin,
board; a poor man's coat
hung on nails; two chairs
for smoke and talk.

Soon the light will fade
to shadow, the bed to shape
and color of sleep.
Soon Munch will carve
his scream. The century will die
into its pictures.

Later, the Great War.
Nothing simple. Nothing
filled with light.

Peacock feathers will scatter,
overstuffed chairs leak bugs
and batting, bric-a-brac break,
old realities disintegrate.

Only this remains: The yellow wall.
The narrow bed. Essential rooms
dim-lit by inner light.

Dutch Interiors

Seventeenth-century Dutch paintings, Seattle Art Museum, 1993

Oak beam, oak table,
pewter bowl, marble tile
scrubbed of sin and scum.
The caged bird sings
and Virtue is a woman
reading in window-seated,
diamond-leaded light.

Among peeled lemons
and pale wine, no Africans choke
in Dutch East India
ship holds, chained to shelves
of dung, phlegm, and blood.
Among lutes and books,
no dying groan
disturbs the varnished light.

What the *I Ching* Said

Modesty. Attend to small things.
A penny
dropped to the floor.
Fingernail clippings.
The tick of morning clocks.
Take little vitamin pills.
Pay the bills.
Water the yew, the philodendron,
the Queen of the Night.
Bow to new light.

Beauty

is a bone of the body,
mystical bone, body's bliss.
A tear. A trope. A turn
of mind, mirage, mind's eye
movies, synapses seeing
lovelies, whether cosmetic

or cosmic. Cosmetic
eye shadow shutters a body
I know, who's seeing
somebody, seeking bliss,
seeking to catch a lover's eye
perhaps the wheel to turn.

And now it's her turn.
Nothing's truly cosmetic.
It's the visual cortex, the eye.
And the eye is the body.
And the body's bliss
is in the seeing.

Exquisite the feel of seeing
stars shooting, a worm's turn,
orange bees and red-ochre bliss.
Color's cosmic, not cosmetic.
We paint our ancient body
to light our ancient eye.

We look with cosmic eye,
sport—or spurn—the All Seeing.
We spin love's body,
oh take our own turn
to pitch coins at cosmetic
counters—to corner bliss.

Or enter no-mind bliss,
our eye a no-mind eye
to beauty, whether cosmetic
or Vedic or fatidic, we seeing
now, Earth's cosmic turn
in a single cell, its carbon body.

Decomposition

Words are bodies whose members are letters.
—GASTON BACHELARD

Body count: cave mouth, river mouth,
bottleneck, fat chance.

Body count: Bring the boys home.
Give the Man the finger.
Have a heart! Shit!

Dear Heart,
I miss your face.

The dead go
from their bodies.
In the grass, a dead crow
shrinks to crow feather,
to feather and bone,
to two brown leaves.

The body dreams the kiss of death.
The body dreams the kiss.

Consider the body's kiss.
Consider the body's sex.
Consider the sex of nuts and bolts.
Consider the cavities of cups.

Consider the body politic,
headstone, footnote,
the naked truth.

Consider giving head.

Consider celestial bodies,
bodies of work, bodies of
water. Consider the bodies
of words: pocked, humped,
fused, broken

like speech, words
penetrating words:
pen, net, rate, rat.

Do the stones at the foot
of the mountain remember
the limbs of trees?

In my dream a stranger
speaks a language
I do not understand.
My body dreams the Man.
The wineglass dreams the wine.
The yellow smoke licks its tongue
upon the windowpane.
I speak in the tongues of dream.

Scavengers

Dear old cat, car-crushed
three hours ago. Already
his nostrils teem with ants.
How changed our fur companion.
Strange, how nature pauses
not at all.

We never saw Susanne, dead
in the woods, blue eyes
open, aristocratic nose pale.
Hunters found her bones
picked clean. Now I know
how soon the buzzards ate
her eyes, how soon the maggots
gorged her lovely mouth.
Perhaps they left her fingers—
thin, musical—till last
so not to miss the breast,
the teeming gut.

Susanne, none of us
is greater than this.
All eat. All end
as food.

Bridge Pose

You arch your bone-back,
rib for strut, femur for bent.
Scapula and foot abut
the mat. The dead load remains
memory's load. The live
load vibrates air and light.
Hawks, gray-winged, lift
your scurried mind to stone-
still gorge and crag. Below,
the unknown river runs
wild and deep and black.

NOTE: A "bent" is part of the substructure of a bridge.

God-Trails

Selah Creek Bridge, Interstate 82, Yakima County, Washington

Concrete arches rise
two crescent moons
above the greasewood gorge.

Twin pikes, eastbound, westbound,
ride the great moonbacks
over sagebrush, bitterbrush.
They crawl with specks of trucks.

The arches, archaic,
mimic ruins of Roman roads.
They lift god-trails
to Rattlesnake Ridge.

Evening throws its shadow curves
on fossil hills, on bobcat and badger,
burrowing owl and balsamroot.

Now let the sun begin
her oath of hawks.

Journey

Shall I tuck a notebook
into your rucksack, a rum cake?
Will you take this gold coin
for luck or river toll
or to pawn or to board
some rogue ship?

You say we will meet again.
You pour bitter dregs, drink
to our works and days.
I drink to your slate-blue eyes.
I drink to the worlds beyond
the world your fingertips trace
on our tabletop. Take my gold.
I will keep my tongue's hoard.
I will dream, as if in pen and ink,
the uncreased map—your face.

Acknowledgments

I thank the editors of the journals in which some of these poems have appeared, at times in previous versions: *Bosque, The Cincinnati Review, Crab Creek Review, Earth's Daughters, Exhibition, Facere Signs of Life Exhibition Catalog, Literary Salt, Margie, Open Bone Review, PoetsWest, Seattle Five Plus One* (anthology), *StringTown, Southern Poetry Review, Women's Review of Books, New Orphic Review*, and *Wandering Hermit Review*.

The late Harold Bond, who taught at the Cambridge (Massachusetts) Center for Adult Education, was my first poetry teacher. To him I am most grateful. I also must thank my poetry teachers in the MFA program at the University of Washington—Colleen McElroy and Heather McHugh.

Bethany Reid and I met in Colleen's workshop more than two decades ago. Her friendship and critical acumen have been indispensible to my life and poetry. Deborah Woodard lent her brilliant mind during two convivial afternoons at Seattle's Herkimer Coffee up on Greenwood, helping me to order the poems. My friend Mitra (Bhikshu Dharmamitra) has nourished the creative work with his perceptive and kindly attention to it. Barbara and J. Glenn Evans are stalwart supporters of Seattle's poetry scene and of my poetry. Esther Altshul Helfgott started the It's About Time poetry reading series twenty-five years ago, thereby nourishing Seattle's rich literary life and my own. Thank you.

My workshop comprising poets, novelists, and visual artists has been going strong for twenty-five years. For a few years we performed as the Seattle Five Plus One, and beyond that we've continued to critique, debate, and cogitate together. I can't imagine how my creative life might have evolved without Gordon H. Wood, Geri Gale, Jack Remick, M. Anne Sweet, Kevin Coyne, Joel Chafetz, Jim Karnitz, Matt Rizzo, Don Harmon, the late Jo Nelson, and the late Irene Drennan.

Saul Slapikoff was the keeper of my poems long before electronic backup devices usurped the task. For his loving support and that of Flora González and Louis Kampf, I am deeply grateful.

All hail to Christine Deavel and John W. Marshall, poets and proprietors of Open Books, Seattle's poetry-only bookstore. Without you, we are pathetic.

I salute the gang at HistoryLink.org, the free online encyclopedia of Washington State history, of which I served as editor for fifteen years. Washington State has more than seven thousand bridges, some of them historic. Most of the bridge poems here grew out of essays I wrote or edited for the encyclopedia.

While teaching at the Taos Summer Writers' Conference, I attended a brief presentation about the University of New Mexico Press's poetry series by editors Elise McHugh and Hilda Raz. I thought, *Wow. To be published by such a stellar outfit, now wouldn't that be something?* And yes, their warmth, professionalism, and love of poetry really is something. Thank you.

Notes

4. *Queen of the Cut*. Tacoma's cable-stayed bridge carries Route 509 over the Thea Foss Waterway. It opened to traffic on January 22, 1997.

7. *Memory's Load*. The Eleventh Street Bridge in Tacoma, Washington, is a vertical lift bridge that spans the City Waterway and opened on February 15, 1913. Murray Morgan (1916–2000) was the preeminent historian of the Puget Sound region. He wrote his book *Skid Road: An Informal Portrait of Seattle* while working as a night-shift bridge tender on the Eleventh Street Bridge. In 1997 the bridge was renamed the Murray Morgan Bridge.

17. *Seasonal Affective Disorder*. The bridge mentioned in this poem is Seattle's Fremont Bridge. It spans the cut that connects Salmon Bay and Lake Union, both of which became part of the Lake Washington Ship Canal when it was completed in 1917. The Fremont Bridge is a bascule bridge, with two leaves that rise to let boat traffic pass. Each leaf has a counterbalance, a heavy weight that dips into the bascule pit when the bridge is opened. Morris Louis (1912–1962) was an abstract painter known for paintings that are numinous in their colors.

18. *High Road Home*. The George Washington Memorial Bridge, known as the Aurora Bridge, carries Route 99 over Seattle's Lake Union. It was dedicated on February 22, 1932, and was the first major highway bridge to be built in Seattle. The Aurora Bridge gained a sad reputation as one from which despondent people have leapt (every jump off this bridge does not result in death, but many do). About 230 people have died jumping off the Aurora Bridge. This was sufficiently disturbing to the increasingly populated neighborhood near and under the bridge that in December 2006 emergency telephones were installed to allow suicidal persons to call for help. In February 2011 the construction of an antisuicide fence was completed at a cost of $5 million. The bridge is an object of monumental beauty. It was designed by Ralph Ober (1871–1931) and has been placed on the National Register of Historic Places. It is a cantilever bridge. Before the center span was set into place, the old tall ships docked in Lake Union or in the connected Lake Washington were towed out. They could not fit under the new bridge and were therefore torched at sea.

22. *Pantoum for a Pontoon Bridge*. The bridge built to span Hood Canal and connect Kitsap Peninsula with the Olympic Peninsula opened on August 12, 1961. It had a long floating section that rested on twenty-three massive, concrete pontoons. (The hollow pontoons were lighter than water when they weren't filled with water.) This type of floating bridge had been designed to span calm lakes and the Hood Canal Bridge was the first to be built over salt water. The misnamed Hood Canal is an arm of the sea subject to tides, storms, and waves that can

reach eighteen feet in height. On February 13, 1979, a severe storm sank the western half of the bridge. It was rebuilt, using new engineering experience gained from oil rigs. It reopened on October 3, 1982.

27. *PTSD Poem.* The italicized line is from T. S. Eliot's "The Waste Land."

28. *Cliffs of Fall.* In 1932 Clark and Cowlitz Counties erected Yale Bridge to span the Lewis River on State Route 503 not far from the town of Yale, Washington. The Lewis River is the boundary between Cowlitz and Clark Counties. The Yale Bridge is the only short-span steel suspension bridge in the state of Washington. The italicized lines are from Gerard Manley Hopkins's poem "No Worst."

29. *Green River Blues.* The Green River Killer, as he became known, murdered forty-eight young women between 1982 and 1998. He dumped many of the bodies in or near the Green River, King County, Washington. On November 5, 2003, Gary Leon Ridgway pleaded guilty to the murders. The prosecution, led by King County prosecutor Norm Maleng (1938–2007) forwent the death penalty in exchange for a complete accounting of the murders and a sentence of life imprisonment without parole. The cooperation enabled victims' families to finally learn the fate of their daughters and sisters, most of whom were prostitutes. The epigraph is from the poem "Ask Me" by William Stafford.

33. *Hot Words.* Irene Drennan (1922–2008) was a Beat poet of Irish and Cherokee descent who moved from New York to the Pacific Northwest and was a member of the team of performing poets The Seattle Five Plus One. The italicized lines are from her poems.

35. *Send Word to Lorca.* The italicized lines are from the poem "Lament for Ignacio Sánchez Mejías" by the poet Federico García Lorca (1898–1936), translated from Spanish by Alan S. Trueblood and included in Lorca's *Selected Verse* edited by Christopher Maurer. In the early days of the Spanish Civil War, during the Fascist uprising in Granada, Lorca was arrested by order of one of Franco's generals. He was driven into the countryside outside Granada and executed.

38. *Visitations.* Susanne Long (1946–1986); Olive Erisman Henry (1895–1987); Regina "Gay" Brown (1943–1961). The epigraph is from the last sentence of *The Bridge of San Luis Rey* by Thornton Wilder.

41. *Mount Tahoma.* Mount Tahoma or Mount Tacoma was the original Indian name of Mount Rainier. The English explorer Captain George Vancouver (1758–1798) named the mountain after his friend Rear Admiral Peter Rainier. Rainier never saw the mountain nor set foot in the United States. Later a long battle erupted over whether to change the name back to Mount Tahoma. Tacoma people wanted to revert to the original name, but a Seattle faction fought to retain the name Rainier. Seattle won.

48. *Love Poem*. This poem was made by using only words used by the French philosopher Gaston Bachelard in an essay he wrote on the masculine and feminine endings of words. This was done with only a small amount of cheating. The epigraph is from Bachelard's *The Poetics of Reverie*.

56. *Dutch Interiors*. This poem was inspired by an exhibition at the Seattle Art Museum of seventeenth-century Dutch painting. The golden age of Dutch painting, which spanned the century, emerged within an economy made prosperous in large part by the Dutch East India Company, founded in 1602. The Dutch East India Company traded in spices and other goods, and in slaves.

62. *Scavengers*. My younger sister, Susanne Long (1946–1986), was a teacher of English as a second language with a master's degree in linguistics. At age thirty-two she developed paranoid schizophrenia, which worsened until she disappeared from a mental-health clinic near our parents' house on July 21, 1986. A nationwide search ensued. Despite our father's search of these deep, tangled, marshy woods with his dogs a number of times, hunters found her dead there on November 7, 1986. It is likely that she committed suicide by ingesting an overdose of the antipsychotic drug Haldol.

63. *Bridge Pose*. Bridge pose is a well-known asana (position) assumed in the practice of yoga. In bridge-engineering lingo, the "dead load" is the weight of the bridge itself. The "live load" is the weight of traffic crossing the bridge.

64. *God-Trails*. The Selah Creek or Fred G. Redmon Memorial Bridge spans Selah Creek on Interstate 82 just north of Yakima, Washington. There is a turnout on the Yakima side, the only good place from which to see this monumentally beautiful structure. When it opened on November 2, 1971, the twin-arch concrete bridge was the longest concrete-arch bridge in North America. Together the two arches form the highest bridge in the state of Washington. The bridge is 1,337 feet long and rises 325 feet above the canyon floor. The arch spans (excluding approach spans) are 549 feet long. The landscape evoked is that of the shrub-steppe ecology of eastern Washington.

About the Author

Priscilla Long is a Seattle-based author and teacher of writing. Her previous books are *The Writer's Portable Mentor: A Guide to Art, Craft, and the Writing Life* and *Where the Sun Never Shines: A History of America's Bloody Coal Industry.* Besides poetry, her shorter works include science, creative nonfiction, and fiction; her science column, Science Frictions, appeared on the website of The American Scholar for ninety-two weeks. Her work has appeared widely in literary journals and her awards include a National Magazine Award. She has been a fellow at Hedgebrook, the Millay Colony for the Arts, and Jack Straw Productions. Her MFA is from the University of Washington. She serves as founding and consulting editor of HistoryLink.org, the online encyclopedia of Washington State history. For more information please visit PriscillaLong.com and PriscillaLong.org.